"3 free resources from Surrogate Mothers Inc"

Access Online at www.FindASurrogate.com

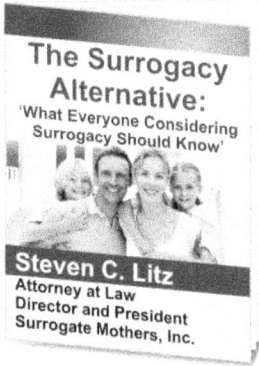

The Surrogacy Alternative:

"What Everyone Considering Surrogacy Should Know."

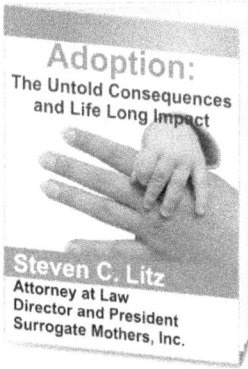

Adoption:

The Untold Consequences and Life Long Impact

The Surrogate Mothers, Inc.

Information and How-To Guide

About the Author

Steve Litz is 51 and has been married to his wife Stephanie, a pediatric dentist, for twenty six years. They have 22 year old twins—their son Brandon, who currently attends Franklin College in Indiana, and their daughter Marika who is studying at the Tisch School of Film at New York University.

Litz received his BA with distinction in English and Philosophy from the University of Virginia in 1981; and graduated from IU School of Law in 1984. He began his law career with the firm of Nile Stanton & Associates, remaining with the firm until it closed in 1986. Since then, he has been in private practice, concentrating in criminal defense and surrogacy. In conjunction with his surrogacy practice, he lectures on the subject throughout the nation.

A member of the Morgan County Bar Association, he served as its president from 2003-2005. He is a member of the National Association of Criminal Defense Attorneys and has served as a public defender since 1993.

In 2008 he received the prestigious Heartland *Pro Bono* Award for service to indigent clients.

When not working, Steve and Stephanie, now empty nesters, enjoy traveling, are passionate about skiing and are skilled ballroom dancers.

Recently, Litz added "author" to his resume with his book, "My Surrogacy Story," which details the many fascinating aspects of matching willing surrogate mothers with clients who long to have children of their own, both those who are infertile and those who may be unmarried or in gay relationships.

ISBN 978-0-615-42317-3

My Surrogacy Story

Over a Quarter Century of the Strangest,
Saddest, Most Rewarding
Experiences of Helping People
Create Families

By

Steve Litz, Attorney

This book is dedicated to my family

and to all of my clients

across the world

who have allowed me

to become a part of their lives.

Steve Litz

Chapter 1

"You should consider yourself lucky; the guy next to you just died."

The most amazing thing about helping create life for hundreds of people from across the world is that it all began with my own almost ending; so before we begin our discussion of surrogacy, I'll tell you about my personal ordeal, an ordeal that led to my advocacy of surrogacy.

***

When you're 18 you think you're invincible. It took only one word to show me that I wasn't. The word was "CANCER", and cancer is a beastly disease.

I was a freshman at the University of Virginia when I noticed a lump in my neck. It was the winter of 1977. Because I ran and played tennis, I assumed it was some kind of muscle strain; but my folks suggested I see a doctor about it during Christmas break. The Chicago physician I saw, as I later learned, knew my diagnosis right away, but simply told me that when I returned to Charlottesville I should see an oncologist about having a biopsy, *"just to be safe."*

I didn't give his advice a second thought until a few weeks later when I awoke in the middle of the night sweating profusely. This was something that had never happened to me before.

I didn't yet know what was going on, but that spurred me to make an appointment to see Dr. Charles Hess, an oncologist and professor of Internal Medicine at the University of Virginia. Dr. Hess had me come to his office right after I called him.

During the examination, Dr. Hess stuck a 3-inch needle into my neck to aspirate some fluid. A few days later he called me back to his office and informed me of his diagnosis. I had Hodgkin's disease.

The diagnosis at first meant nothing to me; but as I was walking back to my dorm room, I stopped at the medical library and looked it up. *"Hodgkin's Disease is a cancer of the lymphatic system that is almost always fatal…"* began the discourse on my ailment. I read no further.

There was no point in reading further. I was 18, and probably wouldn't see 19. I remember very little else that day, except calling my parents and telling them that I was dying. I was totally dazed by what I had learned.

The only problem was that in my haste to find out what Hodgkin's was, I hadn't bothered to look at the publication date on the textbook—I later saw that it was 1959. Thankfully, in the intervening years, the prognosis for Hodgkin's disease had markedly improved.

Dr. Hess didn't exactly laugh, but he did tell me if there was a "good cancer" to have, Hodgkin's was it. It was easily treatable with either radiation or chemotherapy, depending on how advanced it was. The cure rate, meaning the percentage of people who live at least five years (and thereby have no greater likelihood of a recurrence than anyone else in the general population has of being diagnosed with cancer), was around 80-90%. This news was slightly more encouraging than the dour prognosis the ancient medical book had given me, but as yet I didn't know what was involved in determining how advanced my cancer was.

The first test I was given involved sticking a needle in between each of my toes to inject a purple dye that would travel throughout my lymph system. Doctors could then take an x-ray of my body to see where else the disease might be. The difficulty with this test (called a lymphangiogram) was that there was no way to anes-thetize the area in between my toes without sticking a needle in there first. As you can imagine, the crevice between the toes is very sensitive; so the test was a painful beginning to dealing with my illness; but when the results came back, they were okay. *So far, so good.*

The next test was a bone marrow biopsy, where doctors stuck a bigger, hollow needle into my back to extract a sample of my bone marrow. The results of the biopsy came back negative, but the test itself was *excruciatingly* painful. To this day, I cannot watch a television show that features any kind of lumbar puncture. The memory of my own procedure is simply too disturbing to recall.

The final test was a splenectomy—the removal of my spleen. Hodgkin's has an affinity for the spleen; but it's a vestigial organ, like your appendix, so losing it was not a problem. *(Mine grew back— a medical rarity!)* Since I was fit, I bounced back from the surgery quite quickly.

My stay in the hospital was uneventful—other than having to deal with a nurse who, as I was wheeled into the recovery room complaining of pain in my stomach (at the incision site), said, "You should feel lucky; the guy in the bed next to you just died."

And thankfully, the results of the splenectomy also came back negative, meaning that I was classified as type I-B. At this stage, the disease was only in one place above the diaphragm, but I was "symptomatic" because of the night sweats.

Radiation was the course of treatment chosen; and over the next six months, I underwent dozens of radiation treatments, most aimed at the site where the cancer was, a few aimed below my neck as a precautionary measure in case the cancer had spread below the diaphragm and had been missed by the tests the doctors had done.

The radiation made me sick and—toward the end of the treatment—quite tired. Part of my hair fell out on the back of my head. Since I had curly, wiry hair, it was bizarre when it grew back straight and as soft as goose feathers. The only other side effect of the radiation is that it made me sterile—*or so I thought.*

Later, in my senior year at Virginia, I had a sperm analysis done. The doctors were perplexed as to why my count was "0" until they asked me if I had ever been exposed to radiation. They mentioned that in some cases people were known to regenerate sperm, but they were unable to predict whether I would be one of those cases.

I was now 21, and the thought of not being able to have children paled in comparison to the other option of not receiving treatment at all. Besides, since I was going to be a lawyer, I could always adopt if I wanted—at least that was my thought process at the time. My first foray into the world of infertility would prove that idea very wrong.

As a teen, I would never have guessed I would end up specializing in surrogacy. When I was 13, I had read a book by F. Lee Bailey called *The Defense Never Rests*. From that point on, I knew I wanted to be a criminal defense attorney. The idea that someone's life rested in my hands and depended upon my words fascinated and terrified me. It was and continues to be a lifelong challenge, one that strangely enough has evolved into my representation of two entirely different types of people—those accused of crimes who typically are impoverished and uneducated and *have no one else to turn to* and those who are infertile, often come from wealth and pedigree, and *have no one else to turn to.*

It is rare that someone who hasn't committed a crime comes to me and confesses that they're about to break the law. It is rarer still that someone who has never tried to conceive asks for a surrogate. In my practice, no one comes to me first; I am their last resort, their last hope.

I had not anticipated specializing in surrogacy, until I began researching adoption in law school. I quickly learned that, contrary to public opinion, there are very few healthy, white infants available for adoption. In fact, for every baby placed for adoption, there are 50 infertile couples looking to adopt it. This, coupled with increasing numbers of women terminating their pregnancies, couples delaying their efforts to have a child and what for many (single, gay, those over 40, etc.) is the impossibility of adopting, was what led me to begin researching surrogacy as an alternative to infertility, particularly because it was an avenue I thought I might have to travel myself.

As it turned out, I was one of the fortunate ones who did not need to use my own surrogate program to have a child. My wife and I tried for 18 months to conceive. She charted her temperature. She took Clomid to try to regulate her cycle. I gave her shots of Pergonal. (*To be more precise, I tried to give her a shot of Pergonal, but I was so afraid of hurting her that instead of forcefully pushing the needle into her butt, I gently pushed it against her skin, causing her more pain than she ever should have felt, thus ending my shot-giving career before it ever began.*)

Finally, after a year and a half of the least fun sex imaginable (*"Quick, honey, you need to come home right now; I'm fertile!"*), in what I consider to be one of life's great ironies, the same day we found out we were pregnant with twins was the day I found out that my

Hodgkin's had returned and I would not be able to have more children.

This time around, the treatment of choice was chemotherapy; and it rendered me sterile; but going through pregnancy at the same time as chemotherapy allowed me to focus on the positive—on the new lives we were bringing into the world; and while I would never wish on anyone else what we went through, our battle with infertility has allowed me to bring a certain kind of sensitivity to the surrogacy program because I know firsthand how important and life-altering the desire to have a child can be.

I began my career as a lawyer working with a man named Nile Stanton, the greatest criminal defense attorney Indiana had ever seen. Nile welcomed my new area of practice, probably because it was as controversial as he was.

Surrogate Mothers, Inc. (SMI) officially began when I took out a small classified advertisement in *The Indianapolis Star*. At first, the newspaper refused to print the ad; but after discussions with several editors, *The Star* eventually agreed to run the ad, which read:

> **Surrogate Mothers wanted**. Fee plus expenses for carrying a couple's child. Must be 18-35 and previously had a child. Steve Litz, (317) 996-2000.

At the time of the ad, there were only two other surrogate programs in the world. No state had a law addressing surrogacy. Surrogacy was, quite literally, still in its infancy. The uproar that ad created is still being felt today.

* * *

"We are thrilled beyond words to have a child. Surrogate Mothers, Inc. made our dreams come true, and our lives are forever changed because of them."

Miguel and Alicia, Barcelona

Son born 2/92

Chapter 2

"You're nothing but a glorified pimp."

The ad first appeared on a Sunday. Monday morning when I arrived at work I had a surprise. My secretary told me I had a client waiting for me. *(Fresh out of law school, I had no clients. Nile had plenty, but I was far too green to have clients at this point.)* I introduced myself to them and asked how I could help.

"We want a baby," they said.

After fielding about 100 phone calls in the first few days from women who thought they might consider surrogacy, Angie and Mike* chose a young welfare mom named Darlene.

Darlene, who had a son, had experienced a difficult life but was one of the kindest, most-altruistic women I've ever met. Even though she could have asked for a fee of $10,000, she asked for only half that. Because of the craziness that followed Indiana's first surrogacy birth, she was prohibited from receiving even this paltry amount. She eventually became my first secretary and brought empathy to the program as few other women could.

---

* Clients' and surrogates' names have been changed to protect their privacy. All other people are correctly identified, and all stories discussed in this book are 100% accurate.

The fascinating aspect of operating a surrogate program is that it is constantly changing. Just when you think everything is going smoothly, someone throws a curve and you have to start again. In Darlene's case, we faced several obstacles. Initially, Angie and Mike were uncomfortable about meeting Darlene. One evening while they were at a dinner party, Angie relented and gave Darlene a call. They spoke for the next two hours and remained close throughout her pregnancy.

Darlene was artificially inseminated with Mike's sperm and conceived on the first try. At about 10 weeks into her pregnancy, however, she miscarried. I'll never forget telling the couple that she had lost the baby. All of us cried, but Darlene was still committed to helping them and again got pregnant after the next insemination. In May, 1986, she delivered Indiana's first child conceived through surrogacy.

The media frenzy surrounding the birth was intense. Because Angie was not the biological mother, she had to adopt the child. Regrettably, we appeared in front of a judge who had a distinct anti-surrogacy agenda; and he appointed a guardian for the child.

Although the guardian was supposed to be concerned only with the child's best interest, he immediately filed court papers challenging surrogacy. Remember, my clients and Darlene were united in their desire to have Angie adopt. The judge reluctantly granted Angie's petition to adopt the child.

At the attorney's suggestion, the judge determined that surrogacy equated to child selling and prohibited the couple from paying Darlene her fee. Fortunately, the Indiana Legislature disagreed with the judge's view of surrogacy, but the case made front page news. I still remember sitting in front of the television with my wife, being amazed that reporters would want to talk to me about surrogacy.

When I started SMI I figured it would be confined to Indiana clients and surrogates. After Darlene's case made the papers and after AP picked up the story, I was invited to speak to groups from across the country about our program. My clientele expanded worldwide, and we had surrogates apply to us from as far away as Anchorage.

During one radio show, I was asked whether I felt that surrogacy exploited poor women who were doing this just for the money. I responded that the question itself displayed a fundamental misunderstanding about surrogacy. The women in our program have *never* done this for the money. The money is a factor, as it has every right to be; but if someone contacts me and says, "I need $10,000 to be a surrogate," they are automatically rejected.

SMI's surrogates are without question the most generous women in the world. They do this because they love being pregnant, they conceive easily; and they want to give of themselves in a way few women could and even fewer could understand.

Surrogacy also, I have learned, is one of the most empowering things a woman can do. Far from exploiting women, it gives them a sense of worth and independence that no other endeavor could provide. Many of our surrogates come from unstable upbringings. Some have master's degrees. All of our surrogates are guided by altruism.

This was my response to the query about exploitation—the questioner simply replied that he thought I was *nothing more than a "glorified pimp."*

I've never minded debating surrogacy with anyone. There are strong feelings on both sides of the issue. Interestingly, in 26 years of working with people from across the world, I have never encountered *a single person* who has been faced with infertility problems who is opposed to surrogacy.

Perhaps it is the enormity of what a woman is doing that causes people to have such a difficult time understanding how anything but poverty could motivate them. That, I suspect, says more about the critic than it does about the surrogate.

* * *

"We are so thankful that you allowed us to select Helen. She was absolutely wonderful throughout her pregnancy, and she was a perfect surrogate."

Rob and Bonnie, Bangor, Maine

Daughter, born 8/90

Chapter 3

"How long can a man stay in a bathroom?"

As SMI grew, so did its clientele. We began locally, but expanded globally. In the years since SMI was founded, we've been honored to work with people from dozens of countries—ranging from everyday blue collar workers to princes and dignitaries.

In addition to different languages, we've also experienced vastly different cultures. One couple from abroad consisted of Sanje, who was a high-ranking government official, and his wife, who was infertile. Tragically, the culture of their country viewed infertility as a sin. Had anyone found out that the wife was unable to have a child, her husband would have lost his position in government; and there could have been even worse consequences if it was discovered that they pursued surrogacy; so when they came to me, I assured them their confidentiality would be treated with the utmost respect.

Katrina, their surrogate, got pregnant quickly. When she told them the good news, the husband explained that his wife would have to leave the country for nine months so that when she returned with the child no one would know that it was not hers.

Completing the legal procedures for them was particularly rewarding because of the language barrier. We had to translate my English to French for the husband, then to another language for the wife. Happiness is a universal language, however; and everyone, including the judge who presided over the case, was thrilled to be able to assist them. They actually returned to the U.S. three years later and—with the same surrogate's help—had a set of twins born on their second try.

Not all such international arrangements succeed as easily as that couple's did. We worked with a couple from China in 1990. Their surrogate was to be artificially inseminated with the husband's sperm. The couple came to Indianapolis for the procedure, as did their surrogate. As she waited in the doctor's office, the husband was escorted into the *"Masturbatorium"* (that's really what it was called) where the doctor had certain magazines and movies available to help the process along.

After about an hour, his nurse knocked on the door to make sure he was okay. He invited the nurse in; and she discovered him, fully clothed, sitting on a couch reading one of the magazines. Apparently the method by which the doctor assumed he would be producing his sperm was something completely foreign to him. His wife later explained, with some embarrassment, that no one had told him what was expected and he was simply waiting for in-structions. He thought he was in a doctor's waiting room and the doctor was running late.

The irony that the same medical community that enabled surrogacy to thrive is reluctant to endorse it has never been lost on me. Just like 90% of the nation's newspapers that won't run one of our ads, the vast majority of physicians, even those who specialize in infertility, won't assist our surrogates.

We have been fortunate, however, to have a handful of dedicated doctors who have consistently provided excellent care for our surrogate mothers; but in the beginning, the first doctor SMI worked with suffered a heart attack after delivering one of our surrogates, forcing us to scramble to find another physician willing to assist us

When SMI began, surrogacy was simple. A woman was artificially inseminated with a man's sperm; if he was married, after the baby was born his wife adopted the child. Several of our surrogates even did the inseminations themselves, using the "turkey baster" method.

The actual artificial insemination procedure was nothing special. Knowing *when* to do the inseminations was the key, and this was where our doctors' expertise came into play. Getting phone calls in the evening, trying to figure out whether a surrogate's cervical mucus was the right consistency or doing inseminations on weekends or holidays was simply part of their job; and the doctors SMI has worked with over the years have understood the special, if not unique, relationship between the surrogate and the eventual father of the child. Bringing strangers together for such an intimate undertaking is something that requires a special kind of teamwork, and the physicians who help our surrogates to conceive are in a class by themselves.

More special still are those physicians who assist our clients regardless of their marital status or sexual orientation. SMI is the oldest (and only) program in the world that has never discriminated against gay clients. Perhaps because of my background in criminal defense and the fact that I have represented thousands of clients, some of whom have been accused of doing horrific things to children, it has always been my feeling that if I can assist in bringing a child into this world who is much-wanted and will be loved, I have done a positive thing. What possible difference could it make whether the love is given by a man and his wife, two men, two women, or a single man or woman?

About half of SMI's clients are gay. I've been fortunate enough to have dinner at the home of some clients in France where I was introduced to their son; and one of the most beautiful pictures I've ever received from my clients was from two men from California who, in the photo, were on either side of their smiling, completely bald daughter.

In 1990, I attended a conference in New York where I enlarged that picture to poster size. I received more positive comments from that single picture than from any other graphic I've ever displayed. In fact, SMI's website was designed largely by one of my gay clients who attended that conference.

Regrettably, homophobia is alive and well across the world. Although surrogacy is practiced in a few other countries (notably India, but more on that disaster later), surrogacy for gay clients occurs only in the United States; and even in this country it still remains difficult for the partner of the father to adopt. Many states have an outright prohibition on adoptions by gay people; while other states make it quite difficult for gays to adopt, necessitating absurd arrangements where a couple may rent an apartment for a few months solely to establish residency in a state that permits gay adoption. For international clients who happen to be gay, it is next to impossible to get two men's (or women's) names on the birth certificate.

Some countries so discourage surrogacy that if my clients return to, say France, with just the male's name on the birth certificate, they risk tipping off the authorities that the child came into the world through surrogacy. To combat this, if a surrogate delivers a child for my French clients who happen to be gay, regardless of whether she is in fact the biological mother or not, her name must go on the birth certificate. Then, months after the child is born and has returned home, we must terminate her parental rights, leaving the baby's father with sole custody. Even then, things can go awry, as the following story illustrates.

Many years ago, Casey delivered a beautiful girl for two of my clients from Edinburgh, Scotland. They told many of their gay friends about the impending birth and even sent out birth announcements to celebrate. One of their "friends" leaked information about the birth to the British press, and the clients were besieged by reporters who used high-powered lenses just to try to capture a picture of the child.

Casey knitted a blanket for the baby and sent it to them; and one of the reporters actually opened the package, got her address and came to the U.S. to try to track her down. They eventually found her Illinois home and followed her and her own son to school. This unwanted publicity ultimately led to the surrogate and her husband divorcing.

Back in Scotland, the British rags published falsified pictures of the "baby"; and the Attorney General even tried to have the child taken away from my clients. They learned a valuable lesson— your surrogacy is a private arrangement that should probably stay that way. Even your "friends" may be the cause of unnecessary problems once you have allowed them to share your confidential information.

Fortunately, my clients and Casey still stay in touch, although she now sends gifts to a post office box rather than to their home.

* * *

"Our daughter is our life, and if it wasn't for everyone at SMI this would never have been possible. They were with us the whole way, and even helped us to get her British passport after she was born. We will be forever in your debt.

Bill and Louis, Edinburgh, Scotland

Daughter, born 5/06

Chapter 4

The Nuts and Bolts of Surrogacy

So you've read some stories about our clients who have children who were born through surrogacy, and you've heard my philosophy behind the program, but how does it all work? How does someone actually get involved in the program and end up with a child?

There are only two basic requirements for my clients: 1) the desire to have a child (which, in all but the most unusual of cases, is a given) and 2) the inability to conceive on your own without endangering your life or the life of the child. What this latter requirement basically means is that SMI will never work with someone who is capable of conceiving, but simply chooses not to.

Infertility is generally defined as the inability to conceive after six months of unprotected intercourse. Most of my clients try much longer than that, and many try all sorts of technologically advanced medical procedures to assist them. A few, like those women who may have been born without a uterus, know from the outset that they will be unable to have a child; but most spend months, if not years, trying to conceive and thousands, if not tens of thousands of dollars, on various procedures before they finally turn to surrogacy.

SMI has no formal age requirements for our clients; but because of the cost, unless a couple has wealthy parents, most people are in their 30's before contacting us. *(We've worked with some clients in their 60's too, although some of our surrogates would not agree to have a baby for someone who won't be able to play baseball with their teenager.)* The typical client in our program is in their late 30's to early 40's, is a college graduate and is successful and fairly aggressive, both professionally and personally.

As I tell everyone who contacts me, the main reason that many people opt not to pursue surrogacy involves the loss of control over what is customarily the most intimate of decisions. Anyone who hires a surrogate sacrifices much of their decision-making power. As the expectant parent of a child to be born through surrogacy, you essentially trust a stranger with the future welfare of your child. This can be an intimidating proposition, particularly for those accustomed to being in control over most aspects of their lives.

Some clients have wanted to control the welfare of their child to the extent that they wanted me to tell their surrogate when and where she could work, what foods she could eat and where she could travel. Our surrogates value their autonomy, just as my clients do; and we treat our surrogates the same way as our clients— respectfully and honestly. So while my loyalties always lie with my clients since I am their attorney; on occasion, I have to take the surrogate's side when clients' personalities take over and they become too demanding.

The relationship between my clients and their surrogate is critical to the success of the surrogate arrangement. That is why we screen our surrogates so carefully. Initially, before a woman can even qualify for our program, she must be between 18 and 35, she must be a United States citizen, she must weigh less than 200 pounds and she must have delivered at least one child herself.

The rationale for the first three requirements is evident; the reason for previous childbirth is twofold. First, it would be ironic to say the least, if a woman became a surrogate only to discover that she, like my client, was unable to have a child. Secondly, it is my personal feeling that the first child a woman bears should not be one she gives to someone else. It is hard enough to deal with pregnancy, childbirth and postpartum issues for a child you **keep**, let alone one you give to someone else.

Assuming a woman is pre-qualified for our program, we either send her an application or she can fill one out online. If she is married or has a significant other, that person must also complete an application. SMI averages approximately 50 phone calls or hits online weekly from women who may be interested in surrogacy. The first "hoop" a potential surrogate must jump through is that they must send us a refundable $10 deposit; or if they have con-tacted us through our website, they must send a second, confirming email requesting information from us.

Of the women we hear from initially, we never hear from 90% of them again; and that is perfectly fine as far as I'm concerned. If a woman doesn't have the $10 to send in or the time to send us a second email, then I don't want to waste my time on her.

Our applications are long; and we ask as many questions as I have been able to think of about her and her family's medical and social history, again for two reasons: 1) I want the surrogate, and her husband if she is married, to spend several hours reviewing the application; and 2) the more information I can provide my clients, the better informed their choices will be. This application process also works quite well as a filter because for every 10 applications we send out, we get perhaps 5 back.

Once a woman submits an application, I review it; then I interview her over the phone. I try to be liberal in my assessment of the surrogate because I want my clients to have the opportunity to review many profiles of surrogates and have a sense of who is qualified and who isn't. So at this point, I might eliminate only one of the five applicants.

We had a nurse from Chicago, who applied recently, who requested a fee of $50,000. That made my job easy. We never allow our surrogates to do this for the money, although the money is certainly a motivating factor behind the decision to become a surrogate. I love what I do, but that doesn't mean I'd do it for free, and I suspect most people feel similarly about their jobs.

Our psychologist pays careful attention to the surrogate's reasons for joining our program as well. Time and time again we see comments such as "I love my children very much and can understand a little bit what it would be like not to be able to have any, and I want to give someone the gift of life." Then, third or fourth on the list, they might say, "We want to set up a college fund," "We want to put a down payment on a home," or "We want to go on a special vacation." If the reasoning is reversed—if money is the main motivator—they are rejected from the program.

Interestingly, a few surrogate programs, all of which are now defunct, believed that it was actually better to work with poor women who needed the money. According to the thought process of those who ran those programs, such a woman would be less likely to keep a child if she knew she would not receive her fee. This logic, however, displayed an ignorance of the realities behind adoption.

The typical "woman" who places her child for adoption is not a woman at all. She is a 16-year-old welfare mother who obviously is in no position to raise a child. Despite this demographic, half of all women who think they might put their child up for adoption change their minds, proving that financial need has nothing to do with the ability or desire to relinquish a child. If surrogacy had a failure rate of anything approaching this number, there would be no surrogate programs. Surrogacy—at least as practiced by SMI— works because our surrogates are guided by altruism, not poverty.

The concept of becoming a surrogate for altruistic reasons is perhaps the single most confounding concept for the media and the public in general. "How could a woman who does not need the money give up something so precious?" is a question even many of my clients ask. The answer, indeed surrogacy itself, is based on trust. Our surrogates trust that my clients desperately want and will provide for a child. Our clients trust that our surrogates will take better care of themselves when pregnant for them than at any other time in their lives. This mutual trust is what drives surrogacy; and it is what—with one glaring exception—has allowed us to have a perfect track record.

Once a surrogate has been preliminarily accepted into our program, I draw up a profile sheet highlighting her characteristics. The profile, along with profiles of other surrogates, is then shown to my clients along with pictures of the surrogate and her family. The clients review all of the information about available surrogates and make a selection. SMI then calls the surrogate to give her the same kinds of information about our clients that we've given them about her, and she decides if they sound like the type of people (or person) for whom she'd like to carry a child.

Once we have a match, we send the surrogate's application to our psychologist. He contacts her, interviews her over the phone, conducts interviews with her references and submits a brief recommendation regarding whether she should come to Indianapolis for the complete panel of psychological testing.

Before she comes to Indianapolis for the testing, we send the surrogate a DVD which walks her through the entire program. We have found the DVD especially useful because it allows her the chance to see exactly what happens from start to finish from her own home.

The comprehensive psychological assessment occurs over a two-day period. She and her significant other come here and spend an entire the day with our psychologist. He administers a variety of psycho-diagnostic exams, then scores and evaluates the testing. Finally, he interviews the surrogate, gives other in-person tests and ultimately prepares a 15-page report of his findings.

I also meet with the surrogate while she is in Indianapolis to form my own impressions and to answer any questions she may have.

Whereas I try to be liberal in my initial assessment of our surrogates, we've instructed our psychologists to be conservative. I would always prefer to reject someone who is otherwise acceptable than the reverse.

In the 26 years SMI has been in business, our psychologists have rejected about half of the women they've seen. So when all is said and done, about 1-2% of the women who are considering surrogacy actually end up in our program. I'd like to think that's one of the reasons we've never had a case of failed surrogacy. I am certain that the main reason, however, is because our program is run openly. My clients meet their surrogate, they know each other's names and phone numbers, and they are in frequent contact throughout the pregnancy.

Once the surrogate receives the psychologist's approval, contracts are signed. I always represent the parent(s) and recommend to our surrogates that they have their own attorney. About half of the women elect to proceed with a lawyer's assistance, and that is their decision. We do not force an attorney upon them.

After the contracts are signed, we then proceed with the medical procedures. The location where those procedures take place depends on the type of surrogacy involved and which clinic our client chooses. The surrogate, along with my client(s), goes to the selected clinic where doctors either artificially inseminate her or transfer embryos to her. We then wait to see if she is pregnant. If my client is in the embryo transfer program, ideally 2-4 embryos are transferred. Studies have shown that by transferring this number, there is the greatest likelihood that at least one will take. Of course, it is possible that all the embryos could implant. We've had several triplet births and dozens of twin births.

If all four embryos were to implant, the doctors would ask the surrogate to undergo selective reduction—a fancy term for aborting down to two or three fetuses. This request would be made only if both the surrogate and my client had previously indicated they are comfortable with the idea of selective reduction. If either is not, we would never transfer more than two embryos because we would not want either side to make that difficult moral decision unless we knew it was not an issue.

In the beginning of the surrogate's second trimester, we send her and my client the documents needed for us to go to court to establish paternity and/or maternity. If the surrogate has been *artificially inseminated*, her name and the father's name go on the original birth certificate. If she has undergone *embryo transfer* and the husband's and wife's genetic material was used, my clients' names go on the original birth certificate and there is no adoption at all. *If the wife is not the biological mother or the surrogate has undergone embryo transfer with donor eggs,* only the father's name goes on the birth certificate. If he's married, his wife would adopt the child via a stepparent adoption in their state after the child is born; then when the adoption is final, a new birth certificate would be issued with both husband's and the wife's names given as parents.

Regardless of the particular type of legal procedures employed, we notify the hospital about this special arrangement well in advance of the surrogate's delivery, so that my client has the same access to the child as any new parent does and is able to leave the hospital with the baby.

If my client(s) happens to be from another nation, we also provide assistance in getting a passport from their country for the child. The child actually has dual citizenship initially because it was born in the U.S. but has a parent from another country.

In 26 years, with over 400 babies born, this is how the procedure has worked in every case—except one. I've already mentioned that SMI has never had a case of failed surrogacy, a record about which we are immensely proud. We did have one instance, however, where everything broke down; and it will haunt me for the rest of my career.

Marie was a perfect surrogate. She stayed in touch with SMI regularly. She took her temperature when needed. She was at the clinic for every procedure, and she followed the doctors' directions without fail.

My clients, Stacy and John, an unmarried elderly couple, seemed enthusiastic enough when I first met them. Sometimes I have a wonderful relationship with my clients, and other times it is more distant. In this case, I hardly ever spoke to John. It seemed as if Stacy controlled every aspect of their relationship; but as I told myself (and Marie), it wasn't me or my relationship with the couple that mattered; it was more important that Marie felt comfortable with them; and she did—up until she delivered triplets.

Marie called me on a blustery winter day to tell me she had delivered the children. She said she had tried to contact the couple but couldn't reach them, so I called and left a message for them that their children were born and that there were three! That night they went to the hospital where Marie had delivered, and again things seemed fine. But they stayed *only an hour,* saying that they needed to return home to prepare for the arrival of their children; and then they promptly *disappeared.*

The day after the delivery Marie called me, inquiring when the couple would be returning to the hospital. I called them and left another message. They never returned the phone call.

The following day, an understandably agitated Marie called me again. I called my clients again. No response. The same thing happened the following day, and now Marie was beginning to question whether she had made the right choice. A couple of days later, surrogacy's single greatest nightmare came true—Marie decided that since the couple had not contacted her or seen the babies, she was going to take them home with her. Despite my clients' unexplained absence from the hospital and from their children's lives, I begged Marie to give them another chance. She, after all, had never intended on keeping the children. She already had three of her own, and she certainly had no interest whatsoever in doubling her family's size. With no communication from the couple, however, she felt she had no choice but to take the babies home with her.

Finally, upon learning of her decision, the couple decided they would show up at the hospital; but by then it was too late. Marie left the hospital with the triplets, and the legal wrangling then began. The couple (more precisely, John, since he was the father and Marie was not the biological mother) sued for custody. The trial court eventually ruled in Marie's favor, deciding that John was not suited to be the father, given his apparent lack of concern for the children. The judge ruled that it would be in the children's best interest for Marie to be their parent.

The couple appealed the judge's decision; and almost two years after Marie had delivered, she was ordered to return the children to John because, as the appellate court determined, since she was not the biological mother she should never have been allowed to take the children in the first place. Marie, understandably, was devastated. I was devastated. I felt that the court completely ignored the fact that Marie had given her life for two years to the children.

It was not, however, a case of failed surrogacy. Marie never intended to keep the children. She would have never kept them if the couple had shown the slightest interest in them. No, this was a case of failed parenting. I should never have allowed those particular clients to participate in our program, and I'm sorry to say that I did so. I wish I could have predicted their outrageous behavior. I will forever regret that I did not.

I relate this story in such detail to highlight that surrogacy works. This case was an aberration. With this one exception, my clients have consistently demonstrated that they desperately want a child. It is the usual case that the children born to our surrogates, if nothing else, will be the most spoiled children anywhere; *because they are the most desired children anywhere.* Every client I've ever told about this incident is stunned to hear that the couple did not spend every waking moment at the hospital. How could anyone seemingly strive so long for a child only to abandon it once it finally arrives?

Even though I have considered screening my clients psy-chologically, I still have never done so, nor will I. When my wife and I were struggling with our infertility, no one told us we had to see a psychologist before we tried to have a child. Besides, as far as I know, there is no test anywhere that can predict who will or won't be a good parent. All I can ask is that my clients have the desire to become parents and—other than with this one glaring exception— I've never had to question my judgment.

* * *

"My son Joshua just graduated high school. I wanted to thank you again for being there for me, for allowing me to participate in this amazing journey with Lisa, and for the wonderful gifts you've sent Josh over the years. We will never forget you."

Don, Jeffersonville, Indiana

Son, born 4/92

Chapter 5

"You brought what to the hospital?"

Surrogacy has brought me untold happiness. The letters of thanks I receive, many of which are quoted in this book, capture some of the true joy my clients feel when they see their child for the first time, when their son graduates high school or when their daughter walks down the aisle. Every so often, I'll get a thank you note out of the blue from a client who, 20 years ago, had a child through our program. I receive pictures of "my kids" from all over the world; and I put them all in an ever-growing scrapbook as a reminder of the incredible journey this has been; but as much as I absolutely love hearing from past clients, occasionally a case comes around, then stays around, that makes me wish my crystal ball worked a little better.

Henry's ordeal is just such a case. Henry was a 58-year-old single teacher who had never married and had devoted his entire life to children. He was known for his kind ways with his students, but he was famous for his magic tricks. He began his career as a special education teacher and taught in the New York public school system for almost 40 years before deciding he'd like to share his love of children more personally. He was introspective, if not shy, but a genuinely warm and gentle man. His surrogate delivered twin girls in February, 2005 at an Indianapolis hospital.

Henry made the disastrous mistake of going to the hospital with his pet bird in his pocket. The bird had been used in his magic act for years, was trained, vaccinated and completely harmless.

As Henry made his way to the billing office, one of the social workers saw him, stopped to talk to him and realized he had a bird with him. She contacted the department of child services, and they filed papers seeking to take his children from him. What followed was (and continues to be as of the writing of this book) a nightmare the likes of which no parent should ever have to endure.

After Henry had been evaluated by any number of psychologists, social workers, guardians and other child care professionals, it was determined that he posed no threat to anyone, least of all his children. The original judge who handled the case was, however, vehemently opposed to surrogacy. Judge Marilyn Moores not only released information about the case to the press, something later condemned by an Indiana appellate court, she even wrote a letter to the *Indianapolis Star* criticizing my program and suggesting that the United States Attorney General ought to investigate it.

Judges are supposed to remain neutral in the cases that come before them; and if they realize that they are not or cannot be unbiased, they are supposed to have the integrity to remove themselves from the matter. This judge possessed no such quality, and we had to fight tooth and nail to get her off the case. She finally granted my motion to have a different judge take over, and he promptly issued an order keeping the case confidential. Someone broke the law and released identifying information about Henry and his girls to the press, and they printed story after story about them. No one has ever had to answer for violating the law by releasing such information; the reporter who wrote the stories, including one containing a false claim that I had allowed the judge who eventually heard the case to stay at my home in Colorado, was transferred to another newspaper.

Henry's petition to adopt his girls was approved by still another judge; but the State appealed that decision; and in 2009, the Indiana Supreme Court sent the case back to this judge because Henry was not an Indiana resident at the time he asked to adopt his girls. In the meantime, Henry and his twins were living in New Jersey, and the social services organization there also tried to get his girls from him. A judge in New Jersey twice rebuffed those efforts, each time finding that Henry was a loving, doting father and to remove the girls from him would cause them irreparable harm. The Catch-22 Henry now faces is that he needs the approval of the same organization that has twice unsuccessfully tried to take his children from him in order to bring a successful end to his legal situation. His girls, who are now 5, remain without a legal father while two states wrangle over how to handle this case—all because of his error in judgment in *bringing a bird to the hospital.*

* * *

"You are a Godsend to us. We tried to have a child for 5 years and all it brought was frustration. In 5 months since we selected our surrogate, we now are expecting a baby, and we are so excited to start this new chapter in our lives. Thank you. Thank you. Thank you."

Sylvia and Christian, Sydney, Australia

Expecting twins, 1/11

Chapter 6

"Is surrogacy baby selling?"

Surrogacy's ever-changing and intricately complicated legal status is something that very few attorneys have experienced. Because of the myriad of state laws that in some fashion address surrogacy, the public is confused over whether it is legal or not. About half of the states in this country have laws relating to surrogacy. Three states actually criminalize it—New York, Michigan and Washington. We receive requests from women from those states all the time asking if they can be surrogates; but regrettably, the answer is that they cannot.

The state of New York, interestingly, originally proposed regulating surrogacy; but the then-governor was not happy with that decision and commissioned a second study group that recommended outlawing it. Today, if I was to have a surrogate program in New York, I could go to jail for 5 years, lose my law license and be fined $50,000.

Philosophically it is easy to distinguish surrogacy from selling a child. Child selling is criminal in every state. Still, it remains rampant. We are contacted all the time by women who are pregnant and want to know if they can sell their babies. The going rate for a healthy white infant on the black market is around $50,000-$100,000.

No one considers selling their child unless they are in desperate financial straits. They then turn to unscrupulous people who care nothing about them and whose sole goal is to get as much money as possible for the baby. They cannot deliver at a hospital because of the risk of discovery, so most black market births take place with little or no medical care.

Contrasted with baby selling, the typical surrogate in our program is a 28-year-old high school graduate, married, employed and middle class. Most significantly, her pregnancy occurs out of compassion, not mistakenly. She reviews a carefully crafted contract, oftentimes with her own attorney, and her interests are protected. She is screened psychologically to ensure her willingness and ability to participate as a surrogate. At some point the State is involved, either to investigate the adopting parent prior to granting a stepparent adoption or when the couple goes to court to get a pre-birth court order saying they are the parents.

Lawyers are usually involved, and they too are closely regulated. The surrogate's fee averages 15,000-$20,000, a far cry from the baby broker's demands. She is paid for her services of carrying the child, not for the baby itself. One of the ways we make this clear is by our requirement that if the surrogate miscarries, she receives a pro rata portion of her fee. If the child is stillborn, she gets her full fee. This is clearly a financial disadvantage to the couple who longs for a child and enters into the arrangement, but it is the only way for us to write our contracts legally.

The differences, then, between surrogacy and baby selling are numerous and telling. Most states recognize the distinction, which is why most states try to regulate surrogacy in some fashion; but some states (Indiana among them) still send confusing signals to the public because of inartfully drafted laws that really say nothing about the ability to participate as a surrogate or to work with a surrogate.

The law in Indiana, for example, simply says it is against public policy to enforce a surrogate contract. This is a meaningless rule because the enforceability of the contracts is rarely—and in our program has never been—an issue. If a surrogate were to change her mind and try to keep the child, assuming she was the biological mother and could make such a choice, the issue would then be what is in the child's best interest, not whether the contract she and my client signed was enforceable.

Virginia has an absurdly complicated law calling for investigations of both the surrogate and the couple. The results are submitted to a judge who must approve the contract before any medical procedures are performed. The law treats such contracts as enforceable, but no one has ever tried to test it. Almost all states, Virginia included, say you cannot contract away your rights to a child, particularly before a child even exists; so again, a law is created that tries not to offend the infertile community, but which in reality does a disservice to everyone because it is clear to no one.

Nevada and a few other states specifically recognize surrogacy and allow the payment of a fee to the surrogate. These laws, however, say nothing about how much money can be paid, when it can be paid and what happens if it is not or if the surrogate tries to keep the child. Good intentioned? Certainly—but equally inadequate.

Illinois and a couple of other states seem to have gotten it right. Rather than trying to anticipate what might happen in those exceedingly rare cases when surrogacy fails (about two dozen surrogacy cases have gone awry out of about 5000-8000 surrogate births), these states recognize that surrogacy exists and try to accommodate people who avail themselves of it by recognizing that traditional adoption procedures simply don't fit into surrogacy's mold. They allow a couple to administratively obtain a birth certificate with the child's appropriate biological origins. For example, in Utah, if a woman delivers a child through embryo transfer and my clients are the biological parents, rather than having to go to court, all parties can fill out a form at the hospital; and my clients names then go on the original birth certificate.

Even though it has never had a law addressing surrogacy, the state of California usually allows the parties' intentions to control; so if everyone is in agreement, even a gay couple can have *both* men's names on the birth certificate as the fathers. Contrast that law to Florida's which, aside from not even allowing a gay man to adopt, gives the surrogate (if she is the biological mother) a certain period of time to change her mind and rescind her consent after the child is born.

It is no wonder that people have no idea what the legal climate is when they are considering surrogacy. I explain to our surrogates that, after we meet, most of them will know more about surrogacy's legal status than the lawyers in their home state.

The laws on surrogacy can at best be described as inconsistent and at worst throw people into a legal quagmire. It is only because of reputable surrogate programs like SMI that those laws are rarely tested. When they are challenged, when surrogacy goes bad, *no one wins.*

The case that put surrogacy on the map should really never have happened at all. When Mary Beth Whitehead, a New Jersey surrogate who delivered a child for a couple in the late 1980's, kidnapped her child and took her to Florida, all hell broke loose.

I remember very well hearing the chilling tape-recorded conversation during which an obviously distraught surrogate threatened William Stern, the biological father, that he might never see his daughter again. Eventually, of course, he managed to get his daughter back, thereby beginning an emotionally wrenching and financially devastating custody fight.

To no one's surprise, the case made front page headlines for weeks. Each side dragged the other through the mud. We learned about Ms. Whitehead's psychological deficiencies, her spotty work history and her difficult marriage. We learned about Mrs. Stern's struggles with disease and infertility, about the demands the Sterns made on their surrogate and about every nuance of their financial ups and downs.

After months of legal wrangling, the Sterns finally prevailed, only to have Mrs. Stern's step-parent adoption voided and Ms. Whitehead's parental rights restored. The child, given different names by each side, was split in two by the court decisions; and the legal ramifications of the case are still being felt today.

Prior to the *Baby M* case making headlines, only a couple of states had surrogacy laws. Within the two years after, almost 20 states had such rules. Almost all were knee-jerk reactions to the publicity surrounding the case. Legislators did not want to seem unsympathetic to the plight of the infertile, but they also didn't want to ever see a Baby M case in their state. To this day, it is their inability to carefully reason through surrogacy's complexities that accounts for the perplexing jumble of guidelines on surrogacy.

* * *

"I loved being a surrogate! My pregnancy was easy, my couple was super nice, Steve and his team at SMI made me feel special every time I talked to them. I'm pregnant again for a different couple, and I can't wait to see the look in their eyes when I give them their baby!"

Megan, delivered a girl 10/07,

Pregnant again; due to deliver 11/10.

Chapter 7

"I'll try this on my own."

Surrogacy is expensive. We'll talk more about the total investment you'll make a little later on; but there is no question that many people think that in order to save money, they are better off trying to find a surrogate on their own rather than finding their surrogate through a recognized program.

With the advent of the Internet, it is easier than ever to do a Google search and find a woman who is advertising herself as a remarkable candidate. Like most of the Internet, however, there are dangers in trying to navigate it alone. Occasionally, couples do find a woman without our help and everything works out fine. More often than not, though, people contact me midway through their surrogate's pregnancy asking for help; and by then it is frequently too late.

I would never have considered trying to treat my own cancer when I was sick. When people contact me and ask about pursuing surrogacy on their own, I always bring this up.

Why, particularly in an area so fraught with emotions, would you ever want to place your trust in a stranger without the help of people who have seen thousands of women who were not qualified? How can you possibly be objective enough—when you, understandably, so desperately want a child—to decide whether the woman who seems nice enough on the outside is really stable, intelligent and mature enough on the inside to carry your child for nine months, to provide the healthy environment your baby deserves and then relinquish the child to you? Beyond this, there are also the necessary legal papers and proceedings you will need in order to ensure that your interests are protected. These are just a few of the issues I present to people who are considering employing a surrogate on their own.

After hearing my concerns, most people who call me before their surrogate is pregnant realize the risks far outweigh whatever savings, if any, there might be. Some, however, still don't ask for SMI's help; and those are usually the cases that result in the stories we hear about so frequently where surrogacy fails.

Ruth and Dan found their first surrogate online. That relationship ended almost immediately when they set up a time to meet her. They travelled to St. Louis, but she didn't show. When they emailed her to find out what happened, she told them she had found another couple that interested her more than they did.

The couple then found a second surrogate online. This time, they proceeded more cautiously. They called her, did a cursory interview over the phone and set up a meeting with her in Omaha. When they arrived at the given address and rang the doorbell, they were met by a very surprised woman who had never heard of them. She told them someone had stolen her identity, had used her credit cards and was now apparently passing herself off as a potential surrogate using her name. Crushed, the couple returned home and contacted me.

Stories such as theirs are always heartbreaking, but certainly not surprising. At least in their case they had not fronted their "surrogate" any money, as often happens. Unscrupulous women are poised to exploit couples who desperately want a child. Fortunately for this particular couple, all they had lost up to this point was a couple of thousand dollars; but they had also experienced a lot of emotional angst.

When I met with Ruth and Dan, the first question they asked me was whether we guaranteed that their surrogate would not back out. It's a question I'm confronted with frequently and one that *needs to be asked.* More importantly, it *needs to be answered honestly.*

I told them we would put all of our experience to work for them, that their surrogate would be screened psychologically, that I would meet her and give them my opinion of her and that they too would meet her. Only after everyone was on the same page would we proceed.

I also told Ruth and Dan that I could never guarantee that a woman would not back out. (Of course, SMI's track record was pretty good at the time and remains perfect to date.) The couple left my office with three or four top candidates to be their surrogate; but more significantly, they left feeling they could trust the team at SMI.

Two weeks later, they chose Jennifer as their surrogate. We called Jennifer and told her their story, and one could sense immediately that things with her would be different. She was completely sympathetic to their plight and promised that she would never consider doing anything like their first two surrogates had done.

After his initial phone interview of Jennifer, our psychologist confirmed that she appeared to be willing to be a surrogate for all of the right reasons. We brought her here to Indianapolis for the complete testing and learned a number of interesting things about her.

Like a fair number of our surrogates, Jennifer had an abortion when she was younger. It was a time in her life where she was not ready to raise a child, and she made the difficult decision that it would not be fair to the child to be brought into the world when she could not provide for it in the way she felt was appropriate. Jennifer told our psychologist that because of this she would not terminate a pregnancy again. In fact, she said one of the reasons she became a surrogate was to right this perceived wrong that had occurred when she was younger. She wanted to bring a child into the world under circumstances entirely different than her first pregnancy. She now had two children of her own and they were doing fine, but she never forgot the regret she felt in terminating her first pregnancy.

She even theorized that the abortion was what resulted in her first marriage failing. She and her former husband had talked about her feelings concerning the first pregnancy, but she felt he never really understood just how it affected her. Ultimately she decided that she would not share her life with someone who could not or would not empathize with what happened to her. She knew that someone who had *not experienced* the conflicting emotions she felt— knowing that she was doing the right thing but regretting that she had to do it—could ever appreciate what she went through, but she believed that any man who cared enough about her to marry her should at least make the effort.

Because she was unmarried, she struggled financially at times, but she was exceptionally motivated. She had finished college while caring for two young children at the same time and had landed a job at a bank, where she eventually moved up the ladder to become the head of the lending department. She reflected with me on the irony of having struggled for so long, only to find that her hard work had led to a position where she could allay the financial woes of others.

Our psychologist felt, and I wholeheartedly agreed, that Jennifer had the characteristics of a perfect surrogate; she was driven and had a clear picture of herself, was confident, had struggled and overcome; and she believed that her word was her bond.

When Ruth and Dan met Jennifer, they felt similarly. They knew that their past trials were over, and they looked forward to their relationship with her. Jennifer delivered a boy for Ruth and Dan several years ago. To this day, they stay in contact, exchanging holiday cards and pictures of their children. Their story, with Jennifer as their surrogate, was a resounding success even though their surrogate experience began with such failure. Theirs is the classic example of why *do-it-yourself surrogacy is so dangerous.*

That is not to say that all such arrangements don't succeed. I've worked with many clients who have had family members become surrogates for them. I caution my clients in these situations that the relationship between them and their sister, for example, must be a strong one; because the last thing I want to see is the emotional toll surrogacy entails interfere with that relationship.

Tom and Vicky called me when Vicky's sister, Dawn, was a few months pregnant carrying their biological child. As we always do, we sent them affidavits to complete saying that they were the parents and that Dawn was not the biological mother. We then filed an agreed upon paternity and maternity case, seeking a court order affirming what everyone already knew—that Tom and Vicky were the parents. We had obtained these identical orders hundreds of times in states across the country, but this time we encountered a judge who was so myopic that he refused to grant our motion. Instead he ruled that under the state law, the woman who gave birth to the child was the child's mother—period. I challenged the judge to explain how a *man* could show that he was a child's father, and thereby establish paternity, but a *woman* could not. The judge offered no explanation, but refused to alter his ruling.

We appealed the judge's decision, and the Indiana Court of Appeals became just the third court in the country to rule that it was unfair to allow a man to do what a woman could not. They ordered the judge to allow us to show that Vicky had all of the same rights as Tom did and that the couple should be given a birth certificate with their names on it, just as any new parents would be entitled to receive

A case like this actually brought everyone closer together because they were all fighting for the same thing. Dawn gave her sister the ultimate gift, and then had to stand up and fight for her sister's right to be considered the baby's mother.

When the case was finally over, it was enormously gratifying to see the three of them walking hand in hand from the courtroom, knowing that together they had brought a new life into the world and that even the ruling of the original judge had not been able to prevent them from giving the child his rightful name and place with his parents.

I wish I could say that all such arrangements had happy endings. Sometimes there is such discord between the couple and their surrogate that the pairing is doomed from the start. This is another reason why I prefer to be involved with the client from the beginning. While some of my clients may not like to hear my feelings that the woman they've chosen is not right for them, most trust my expertise in gauging whether there is a personality conflict or not.

When Jamie contacted me, she was already pregnant for a couple that had located her themselves. Usually I'm contacted by the couple first; but in this instance, the surrogate called and asked for my help because she felt that the couple was so overbearing that she wanted nothing to do with them. I knew right away that the only way this relationship would be salvaged was if the couple accepted the fact that Jamie's feelings, legitimate or not, were all that mattered. She was clearly hurting, frustrated and unhappy—the worst possible state of mind in which to be pregnant, let alone to be pregnant for someone else.

Jamie had told me that the couple had gone so far as to contact her while she was on vacation and demand that she switch hotels so they could oversee where she was staying. When she refused, they contacted the hotel manager and threatened him, saying that if he didn't ask her to leave, they would contact the police. Not wanting to be in the middle of a situation he didn't understand, the manager asked Jamie to relocate; and she was understandably furious.

I've encountered all types of people in the quarter century that I've been doing this, but this couple was without question the most demanding and imposing of any I'd seen.

I told Jamie that I would try to reason with them. When I called them, it immediately became apparent why she was so upset. The couple screamed at me that I had no business interfering in their lives and that they could treat her however they wished. I suggested to them that I was not at all trying to interfere; I was simply trying to see if I could help them avoid the worst-case scenario where the surrogate refuses to give up the child. I even went so far as to suggest to them that I would be happy to arrange a meeting between them, Jamie and a counselor of their choosing so that each side could air their feelings about the other. They wanted no part of it.

I had to call Jamie and tell her the disappointing news, and I asked her if perhaps she could try to accommodate them for just a little while longer until she delivered. She initially agreed, but said she would only talk to them through a third party. When I tried to convey this to them, they were madder than ever and told me Jamie would be hearing from their attorney. The situation was rapidly spiraling out of control, and I felt that I had somehow done more harm than good. I told Jamie that I would be there if she needed to talk to me; but the couple obviously felt that I was their antagonist, so it would be better if she found someone else to help her.

The couple went through three different sets of attorneys, all of whom initially sent letters to Jamie then promptly told the couple they could no longer represent them because they were so unreasonable in their demands. Jamie delivered a child last year; and sadly the case is still in litigation, the couple demanding that she turn over the baby and Jamie continuing to assert that they are not fit to parent the child because of their neurosis in dealing with her.

This case again highlights why using a surrogacy program is so critical. If we encounter clients who feel the need to control every situation, we can at least caution anyone considering acting as their surrogate that they need to prepare themselves for a trying pregnancy. If someone knows in advance that their situation is going to be difficult, they will be much better prepared to address it.

Of course, we can't be perfect; and sometimes in our pairings, we've had couples and surrogates who have simply not gotten along; but—and here is the key—we are at least in the position to communicate with each side *before* the surrogate conceives and to suggest that since the arrangement is not working, a new surrogate should be chosen. SMI tries its hardest to ensure that we never have a surrogate who dreads working with her couple or *vice versa*. That is a recipe for disaster, as Jamie and her couple so amply demonstrated.

Closely linked to the dangers of pursuing surrogacy on one's own is the likely harm in trying to cut corners with choosing an agency. Surrogate programs have come and gone over the past three decades. There are only three programs that exist now that also were around 25 years ago, SMI being the most notable. Part of the problem is that surrogacy is an unregulated industry. Nothing prohibits a woman who has no qualifications from opening a surrogate program, *with no oversight*, out of her garage—something that has literally happened many times in the past. I always encourage prospective clients to ask for references, contact the Better Business Bureau and ask how many babies a program has had before committing to a program. The only thing worse than trying surrogacy on your own is working with a "program" that has no credentials.

A spate of surrogacy programs from India have cropped up recently. These programs typically advertise a "complete package" for $25,000. I've spent many hours discussing these facilities with clients; and not surprisingly, the risks are enormous. Many people have told me about traveling to India, only to find that the surrogates available are in desperate poverty, frequently have never had a child themselves and often are uneducated minors whose parents aren't even aware of what they're doing.

The idea that someone would travel to a foreign country to hire a surrogate whose background is not investigated, where they have no legal representation, where the pregnancy goes unmonitored and where the doctors have little experience in dealing with artificial insemination and even less with embryo transfer, would be laughable if it were not so serious.

Yoshi, a single man from Israel, explained to me that when he went to India to work with a surrogate program, he walked into a filthy office and was met by a man who didn't speak English. He was shown a book of pictures of women and urged to select one in particular, whom he later learned was already pregnant by her husband and was trying to sell her child. The owner of the program tried to get him to deposit $25,000 in cash up front.

Fortunately his warning signals were on high alert and he left the facility quickly. He then came to us. We arranged to have a limousine pick him up at the airport. We had previously asked him if he would feel more comfortable with a Hebrew translator being present, but he said his English was fine. I explained our program to him in detail, gave him a list of references and the opportunity to review all of our profiles of surrogates (about 50 at the time). He was welcome to take copies of his favorite profiles home with him.

At SMI, we never rush our clients or attempt to "nail down" the cash at the outset. We don't even allow our clients to sign a contract with us the day they visit me. There is simply too much information to digest during our initial meeting to do so. I often say that because the demand for a child is innate, many of my clients would choose a surrogate more quickly than they would buy a home; and that just doesn't make sense to me.

Yoshi was stunned at the difference between our program and what passed itself off as a surrogacy program in India. He left feeling comfortable, knowing we would be ensuring that his interests were protected. As he left, he thanked us for showing him the dangers that could have befallen him had he opted for the "fast-food" version of surrogacy.

* * *

"I cannot tell you how grateful I am that I came to SMI for a child. After a couple of failed attempts at finding a surrogate myself, SMI handled everything professionally. Just 15 months after contacting them, I now have the son I've always dreamed of. Thank you from the bottom of my heart."

Yoshi, Tel Aviv

Son, born 11/07

Chapter 8

The Tragedies and the Triumphs

For every heart-wrenching story of miscarriages, stillbirths and failed IVF cycles that lead my clients to come to me, there are heartwarming tales of multiple births, miracle babies and incredible generosity in the face of enormous odds. These positive outcomes are what make what I do so rewarding. What follows is a compendium of anecdotes about happenings that have, over the years, always kept my program fascinating and serve as constant reminders that no two surrogacy arrangements are ever the same.

Surrogacy, I have learned, is a hugely empowering under-taking. Aside from the incredible joy that our surrogates bring to others, they also receive rewards beyond compare. Their fee, as virtually all of them will tell you, turns out to be one of the least important benefits they receive. Many of our surrogates come from single-parent or divorced families. Many have been through divorces themselves. Unexpectedly, most say that after their experience as surrogates, they have a newfound sense of self-confidence, often for the first time in their lives. This can occasionally surprise and disappoint their husbands, who—until this awakening of their spouses—enjoyed their status as undisputed heads of their households. For Cindy, our third surrogate ever, this sense of empowerment led to a shift in her whole lifestyle.

Cindy grew up in an abusive childhood with an alcoholic father and a cowering mother. Unfortunately, her marriage paralleled her upbringing. She found herself in the same cycle of violence that characterized her youth. Her husband seemed entirely supportive to our psychologist; and, in his own way, I think he did support her throughout her pregnancy for our client; but because her couple showered her with praise, Cindy grew emotionally stronger than at any time in her life.

Cindy began to realize that she deserved to be treated as an equal. After she delivered, she made it clear to her husband that she would no longer tolerate his domineering attitude. He in turn recognized the change in her and couldn't handle it. She attributes her divorce to her growth through surrogacy.

Incidentally, about two years after she divorced, she remarried; then she delivered another child through surrogacy for us. She and her husband recently celebrated their 20th anniversary.

To describe surrogacy as an emotional rollercoaster is an understatement. Our clients are cautious at first, hoping their surrogate conceives. When they find out the good news, they are ecstatic. That immediate rush of happiness turns to conservative optimism as the pregnancy progresses.

I always send my clients a congratulatory letter after we learn of their surrogate's pregnancy, but I also suggest they not decorate the nursery just yet. Our surrogates miscarry at a rate slightly lower than the general population, but about 1 out of 7 pregnancies ends in miscarriage. When this happens to those in our program, it is doubly devastating because our surrogates always feel guilty that they were unable to carry the child to term, which in turn makes our clients feel even worse than they already did.

Lyn, a surrogate from Ohio, had a perfect pregnancy for Miguel and Laurant from France. They came to visit her twice while she was pregnant, and they all got along like the best of friends. She sent them ultrasound pictures after every doctor's visit. Then, three days before she was due to deliver, a factory about a mile from her home had an explosion that knocked her across the room. She ended up delivering a stillborn child the next day. Everyone was crushed; but after waiting three months, they decided to try again. She conceived after the first try, delivering a boy and a girl for them 8 months later.

Colin and Katherine came to the United States from Australia. Katherine had herself borne their 2-year-old son; but after the delivery, her uterus had failed to contract. She had undergone an emergency hysterectomy, barely surviving the surgery. Since she was still in her twenties, she was a perfect candidate for embryo transfer. Geneva, their surrogate from Wisconsin, conceived triplets after the first try.

Because I grew close to the couple, my wife and I invited them to stay at our home when they returned to the U.S. We spent a wonderful week together just before Thanksgiving. The day before the holiday, their surrogate, now 11 weeks pregnant, called them and said she was bleeding. She was checked into the hospital.

That night she lost one of the babies. Two days later, she miscarried the other two.

Colin and Katherine were crushed. She had survived emergency surgery only to find out she would never have children again. Their efforts at embryo transfer were immediately rewarded, threefold, only to lose all three children. They were too spent emotionally to try again, and they returned home to their son. It was a heartbreaking end to their journey.

Graham, a psychology professor at the University of Oregon, contacted us in 1995. He had lost his son in a car crash three years earlier, but he was emphatic that his desire for another child was not so he could replace his first son, but because he felt he had so much love to give and wanted to share those feelings again. From time to time, we're contacted by people in similar situations; and I can usually tell immediately whether someone is doing this just to have an heir or because they really want to parent a child again. I had concerns about Graham but decided that his goals seemed genuine.

"Allowing" a client to participate in our program has always been a bit of a philosophical struggle for me. I never want to be perceived as playing God, but at the same time I believe I have an obligation to ensure that the children our surrogates deliver go to good homes. Although it is exceedingly rare, there have been instances (none in our program) where a child born to a surrogate was abused. There was even a case in Pennsylvania, many years ago, where a single man was arrested and charged with child abuse, an unthinkable end to his surrogate's gift.

There have been only a handful of clients that I have decided were not suitable for our program. One woman, as it turned out, was capable of having a child but for professional reasons decided she didn't want to do so. Another couple was in their 70's, and I felt that was just too old. A third couple was so demanding that I knew none of our surrogates would feel comfortable working with them.

These are tough calls for me. If a potential client really wants a child, I am very reluctant to deny them the opportunity. There must be a truly glaring issue that leads me to think that it would not be in any child's best interest to be raised by the client. Fortunately, I have not had to exclude more than a handful of clients in our 26 years.

Graham, the professor who had previously lost his son, in spite of my original misgivings, turned out to be one of my most gracious clients. He flew to almost all of his surrogate's OB visits. He called her every week to see how she was doing and to thank her for agreeing to carry his child. He even sent flowers to her parents to thank *them* for having such a wonderful daughter. At the hospital he brought her a diamond bracelet. He had a limo waiting to take her home after she delivered. After sending us one of the most sincere thank you notes I've ever received, he also sent us a beautiful framed picture of a mother and child. He continues to send us periodic updates about his child, who is beautiful and thriving. I was honored and thrilled to have worked with him.

* * *

"I delivered a baby for Ron and Joe almost 20 years ago. I just met their daughter, and it was a thrill. I remember how I felt when I delivered, and those feelings resurfaced when I saw her again. Other than having my own child, it was the greatest experience of my life."

Tasha, San Francisco, CA

Delivered a girl, 4/91

———

"Tasha was a joy! We stayed in touch with her throughout the years, and we just had our daughter meet her. We were a bit nervous about the meeting, but it went so wonderfully that we regret not doing it sooner. Steve was the most caring attorney (I know it sounds corny), and the experience wouldn't have been the same without him."

Ron and Joe, Los Angeles, CA

Daughter, born 4/91

Chapter 9

"I can't afford surrogacy."

Other surrogacy programs quote total fees as high as $125,000. As an attorney, I have to justify my fees based on the approximate time I'll spend with any particular client. I also factor in my expertise, the quality of my work, my years in practice and the value of the services I provide. In SMI's program, your total investment in surrogacy will run around $60,000-$70,000. This assumes two important criteria: 1) that your surrogate's fee is around $15,000-$20,000 and that she has insurance covering the pregnancy and 2) that she conceives after the first attempt.

Since almost all of our surrogates' fees fall into this range and since they almost all have insurance, the first of these two assumptions is usually not an issue. Whether she gets pregnant after the first try is nature's call. The majority of our surrogates do. For some it takes longer. Some don't get pregnant at all. *(I should mention, however, that in our program you are always free to choose a second surrogate if your first does not conceive.)*

If you choose a surrogate from Albuquerque, and it takes her 8 months to get pregnant, I will have obviously underestimated the medical and the travel expenses. If things go as they typically do, however, this is an accurate, all-inclusive total. It covers *all fees*—

medical, legal, travel, insurance, daily allowance, maternity clothing—everything necessary.

Here's how the finances work: at whatever point you select a surrogate and she agrees to work with you—in other words, once we have a confirmed match—you make an initial $20,000 deposit. From it, four things are withdrawn immediately. The first is our psychologist's fee of either $1600 if your surrogate is single or $2000 if she is married. Secondly, you pay for your surrogate's travel to and from Indianapolis. If she's local, that could be nothing. If she's from farther away, it might be $1500 or so. Thirdly, your account is charged a $5000 advertising/marketing fee. *(This is what it costs SMI for each woman available in our program. At any given time, we average around 50 available surrogates. We try to have as many women available as possible, but as explained in Chapter 4, finding qualified surrogates takes a lot of time and effort.)* Finally, the first part of my fee, $10,000, is withdrawn. This initial withdrawal is nonrefundable once you sign a contract with your surrogate.

If you never sign a contract with a surrogate and you decide to drop out of the program, the legal fees are refunded in full. This has happened to us twice in 26 years. In one case, the wife of the couple ended up conceiving after they selected a surrogate. If you recall, we don't work with people who are fertile; but occasionally there is no medical explanation for a couple's inability to conceive; and in this one case, apparently all it took for the wife to regain her fertility was selecting a surrogate. In the second instance, one of the males in a gay relationship was diagnosed with acute leukemia, and they withdrew from our program.

From the $20,000, then, about $17,000 is withdrawn immediately. The remaining money is enough to cover a variety of miscellaneous costs such as:

- You pay up to $300 for your surrogate's attorney, if she has one, to review the contract with her. I've tried to write the contract using plain English, unlike the way lawyers usually write; but if your surrogate has her own attorney, you pay for him or her.

- Anytime your surrogate travels, she receives $100/day for each day she's away from home. This $100 is designed to cover three things that the contract between you and she specifically excludes: child care, meals and lost wages. We used to reimburse for these things, but it became a record-keeping nightmare. So, when your surrogate comes to Indianapolis for the weekend for the psychological testing, she is paid $200. If she travels to Portland for the embryo transfer and is gone a week, she gets $700.

- She takes out a $100,000 term life insurance policy. The reason for this is to protect her family if she were to die due to the pregnancy. The insurance costs about $200/year; and if she hasn't delivered by the time it expires, it's renewed for a second term.

- At the beginning of her second trimester, we provide $500 to her for maternity clothing. She may use this for anything she wishes, but it is earmarked for maternity clothing.

When your surrogate conceives, you deposit her fee, which again averages $15,000-$20,000, with SMI. Other than the initial deposit, this is the only time we tie up a great deal of your money. The reason for this is simple—if my client(s) were to die before their surrogate delivers, I want to be sure that her fee is in escrow. Along those lines, the contract you sign with her has a blank where you appoint a guardian for your unborn child. You must also have a will in force before your surrogate conceives that includes a similar provision in the event of your untimely death.

Your surrogate's fee is held for her in SMI's escrow account—with few exceptions—until she delivers, at which time we send her a check. Even though we make it clear to our surrogates that, once the contract is signed, that is the method by which we distribute her fee; occasionally, the unexpected happens. For various reasons, some of our surrogates ask for part of their fee while they're pregnant; and I have no problem with this request. Were your surrogate to lose the child, she would receive a pro rata portion of her fee anyway; and since you are paying her for her services of carrying your child, we never object to a woman receiving her fee as the pregnancy progresses.

We've had surrogates who had to be placed on bed rest during the pregnancy, who then received part of their fee even though they hadn't asked for it earlier. We had one surrogate whose home burned down while she was pregnant, and she needed financial assistance because of this misfortune. Another woman's son needed extensive surgery, and she needed part of her fee to cover the uninsured portion of his medical expenses. Like many other aspects of surrogacy, even though we've been through it hundreds if not thousands of times, unanticipated things sometimes occur that justify deviating from the contract in this manner.

Three months after she conceives, when we go to court and get the pre-birth court order, you add the balance of my fees to the account ($5000). Even though we have figured the medical expenses into our all-inclusive total, many of my clients pay this directly to the clinic. In the embryo transfer program, those costs are around $15,000 for each *fresh* transfer. We prefer to do fresh transfers because the success rates are higher; but if there are extra embryos available after the first transfer, they will be frozen and can be used for subsequent procedures if your surrogate doesn't conceive on the first try. Each frozen transfer will cost about $2000, which is also what each artificial insemination runs.

Every month we will email you an accounting. Every quarter we will send you copies of the checks we wrote, along with a statement showing the activity in your account for the previous three months. So, for example, at the end of August you might get a statement that contains an entry saying, "$55—Jane Smith, travel expenses." Then at the end of September, you'd receive a copy of the check we wrote to Jane, with a notation that might show data such as "$20—parking; $15—ovulation predictor kit," or something similar.

If your account drops below a couple of thousand dollars, we will ask you to deposit more money. We try to have the account as close to "0" as possible, but at the same time with sufficient money to cover all expenses. We do not allow our clients' accounts to go in the red. If your account does not have enough money in it to pay for the costs associated with the program, everything comes to a screeching halt. We will never surprise you by demanding money one day for expenses the next, but the responsibility to ensure that your account is properly funded is yours.

I have always tried to work with those clients who need financial assistance with surrogacy. I have, on occasion, agreed to delay the withdrawal of part of my fee. We've rearranged the timing of the various deposits to help people. We also have a structured financing program in place, both in house and through a medical financing company, to assist clients who do not initially have enough money to get started. As far as practically possible, I never want to deny someone the opportunity to have a child because they are a few thousand dollars short.

Our surrogates feel the same way about the money. We've even had two women do surrogacy for free for complete strangers. Deborah, from Terre Haute, Indiana, agreed to carry a couple's child and asked for nothing in return. Because of her incredible generosity, we tried to make Deb available only to those clients who truly were unable to afford a surrogate's fee.

The couple that actually chose her had been foster parents for years, and finally decided they wanted a child of their own. They came from simple upbringings, were blue collar factory workers and lower-middle class. They just did not have enough money to participate in our program until Deb came along. With her altruism, they were able to pay the medical expenses as well as SMI's reduced fee. Deb delivered a boy for them in 1993. They surprised her a year later by giving her $10,000 they had scraped together as a token of their appreciation. Even though she tried adamantly to refuse it, eventually she agreed to accept the money and—in the ultimate show of mutual affection—purchased two savings bonds, one for her daughter and one for their son.

* * *

"Although it was a struggle to come up with the money to pay for this, we are so grateful that you allowed us to stagger our payments. We would never have been able to afford some of those other 'boutique surrogacy' programs, but your kindness has allowed us to have our miracle baby."

Ken and Darla, Ironton, West Virginia

Girl, born 12/00

Chapter 10
Final Thoughts

As of the publication of this book, SMI has had children born in 40 states and 20 countries. We've had a woman from Anchorage, Alaska deliver for a client from Spain. We've had a surrogate from Pittsburgh deliver for a client from New Zealand. We've had one sister deliver for another. We've even had a daughter deliver a child for her mother (blurring the definition of what it means to be a mother). We've helped hundreds of straight couples, single and gay men, and single women from across the world. We've had almost fifty twin births and three sets of triplets.

We've worked with everyday people who have everyday jobs and also with dignitaries and royalty. Lawyers, doctors, factory workers, psychiatrists, stockbrokers and plumbers have all been our clients. We've seen people in their twenties to people in their sixties become parents. We've had surrogates on welfare and surrogates with masters' degrees deliver for us. What every single one of my clients has in common is that, through no fault of their own, they've been deprived of the fundamental right of having a child. They share a common bond because they have a common goal—to give their love and share their lives with a new being.

What every single one of our surrogates has in common is that they are, without debate, the most altruistic women in the world.

They love being pregnant. They have easy pregnancies. They feel more alive while pregnant than at other moments in their lives. They give of themselves in a way few others understand and even fewer could. Their reward comes from seeing the overwhelming gratitude in my clients' eyes when they are handed their baby, a child who without their help would never have existed.

To those who condemn our surrogates, my reply is that it is unfortunate that they are unable to understand the meaning of true compassion and ironic that they would pre-judge someone just because they can't imagine doing something so selfless.

To those who condemn my clients, suggesting that they could simply adopt a handicapped child rather than spend so much money to have a child of their own (as the judge in our first surrogacy case believed), my answer is that it is unfair to relegate adoption of any child, special needs or not, to those who are infertile. No one suggests to fertile couples that they should adopt rather than have a child of their own, so why make infertile couples take that route first? Adoption can be a wonderful benefit for everyone involved; but it should be a matter of choice, not mandated by the opinions of others.

To those who condemn surrogacy, my response is that they have never had to suffer through the pains of infertility; they have never had to wonder whether they'd ever get to hold a tiny hand in theirs or whether they'd ever get to experience the thrill of having a child run up to them at the end of the day screaming, "Mommy!" or "Daddy!"

Surrogacy has brought so much joy to so many couples and individuals from so many countries that, in my mind, it clearly is a universal good. Can it be complicated? Of course. Can it fail? It certainly has; but with a success rate of 99%, it is vastly more reliable than adoption. It affords people more control than adoption; it is done out of love rather than necessity; it is planned, and it is regulated.

I have been blessed to have worked with amazing women, brilliant doctors, and even the most proficient staff one could ever ask for. I've been privileged to meet people from all over the world who come to tiny Monrovia, Indiana, in search of something the vast majority of the population takes for granted. I've been moved to tears to see the joy on my clients' faces when they hold **their baby** for the first time. I've been angered beyond words at some of the criticism leveled at my clients and, occasionally, at me. Throughout it all, though, I continually return to what got me started in surrogacy—my own desire to have a child. In reflecting on almost 30 years of trying to fulfill that desire for others, I've concluded that there is simply nothing I could imagine doing that ever could compare to surrogacy. My children are my life and, more than anything else, I've been honored to be able to be a small part of giving that indescribable gift to so many others.

Surrogacy offers those unable to have a child themselves the only opportunity (short of going out and buying a baby) to gaze into their newborn's eyes and be able to say, as one of my clients so tenderly did, "Although I could never carry you under my heart, I always carried you *in my heart.*"

End

Appendix 1

SURROGATE LAWS
in Various States

Below is a summary of the laws across the United States that in some fashion address surrogacy. Note that only 3 states: New York, Michigan and Washington criminalize paid surrogacy. If a woman is a resident of one of those states she cannot be a surrogate even if she agrees to deliver in another state if she is accepting a fee. If you have questions about the details of a law in a specific state, you may always contact us or speak to a lawyer in that state. Generally, the law in the surrogate's state of residence is that law that controls; so even if you are from one of the states where surrogacy is illegal, that imposes no roadblock to your ability to work with a surrogate from a different state. Note that internationally, almost every country except Israel and India prohibits surrogacy.

1. **ALABAMA**: Surrogacy is exempted from prohibition of non-licensed child placing agencies. This means that someone could have a surrogate program there. The law says nothing about enforceability of contracts, surrogate fees, custody, etc.

2. **ARIZONA**: Prohibits entering into or assisting in formation of ANY contract; says the surrogate is mom and entitled to custody and if married her husband is rebuttably presumed to be the father. This law, interestingly enough, was declared unconstitutional in 1994 because it violates the Equal Protection Clause of our Constitution; but it has still remained on the books.

3. **ARKANSAS**: Says wife of couple is presumed to be the mom in surrogate case, whether surrogate is single or married. A pro-surrogacy law that has been abused by some lawyers who have actually asked surrogates to travel to Arkansas to deliver. We would never make such a request.

4. **FLORIDA**: Prohibits contracting for sale of custody or parental rights; allows payment of living expenses; gives the surrogate 7 days to change her mind; prohibits programs. Says gestational surrogacy okay. A strange mix of pro-surrogacy but anti-surrogate program statutes.

5. **ILLINOIS:** Recognizes gestational surrogacy; provides admini-strative mechanisms to get bio parents' names on birth certificate. A very pro-surrogacy law.

6. **INDIANA**: Says surrogate contracts void and to enforce them is against public policy but says nothing about the ability to enter into them. Another ambiguous law that has never mattered even when both the surrogate and the client are from Indiana.

7. **IOWA**: Surrogacy exempted from child selling statutes. Every state has laws making selling a baby a crime; Iowa recognizes that surrogacy is different and allows payments to surrogates.

8. **KENTUCKY**: Prohibits advertising; prohibits programs. Pro-hibits contracts for money where payment is for a woman who is artificially inseminated and agrees to termination of parental rights. Again, a state with a law that really makes no sense since, at least in our program, the surrogate's fee is never paid to her in order to secure her agreement to terminate her rights.

9. **LOUISIANA**: AI surrogacy contracts void. Like Indiana's law, Louisiana makes surrogacy contracts unenforceable, which is irrelevant since enforceability of the contract is never an issue.

10. **MICHIGAN**: Prohibits programs; criminalizes PAID surrogacy (1 year in jail; $10,000 fine for participant; 5 years, $50,000 fine for broker). One of the worst laws in the country, it was created in response to a now defunct surrogate program that had all sorts of problems.

11. **NEBRASKA**: Contracts void, but gives biological father all rights and obligations otherwise imposed by law. Another schizophrenic law that tries to be sympathetic to infertile couples but at the same time tries to get those couples to go elsewhere to do surrogacy.

12. **NEVADA**: Allows payments to surrogates.

13. **NEW HAMPSHIRE**: Creates extensive mechanisms for pre-conception approval of contracts but prohibits programs. An absurd law that no one has ever used.

14. **NEW MEXICO**: No payment of money to surrogate, but surrogacy itself permissible.

15. **NEW YORK**: Criminalizes PAID surrogacy ($500 civil fine for participants; $10,000 fine for brokers; 2nd offense is felony); prohibits programs. Strangely enough, when NY first considered enacting legislation on surrogacy, the recommendation was to allow it. They later made it illegal but have never enforced the law even as to surrogacy programs in NY.

16. **NORTH DAKOTA**: Contracts void, SM is mother; husband is father, if SM married; but allows payments to surrogates. Another example of a law with grossly conflicting messages.

17. **OHIO**: Recognizes surrogacy and exempts it from their laws that say if a man donates sperm to someone other than his wife, he is not the father.

18. **OKLAHOMA**: Child born from egg donation considered to be child of birth mother if husband and wife consent to donation (rebuttable presumption).

19. **OREGON**: Same as Iowa; exempts surrogacy from child selling statutes.

20. **SOUTH DAKOTA:** Allows couple's (husband's?) name on birth certificate. Unclear if this applies to AI program as well, but still a pro-surrogacy law.

21. **TENNESSEE**: Recognizes that surrogacy exists but goes no further.

22. **TEXAS**: Recognizes gestational surrogacy and enforceability of contracts.

23. **UTAH**: Recognizes gestational surrogacy; has scheme for validation of contracts. Utah used to have one of the worst surrogacy laws in the country, but several years ago did an about face and now has a good law.

24. **VIRGINIA**: Like NH, has extensive mechanisms for preconception approval of contracts; prohibits programs; recognizes surrogacy but says provisions for payments to surrogate void and unenforceable.

25. **WEST VIRGINIA**: Surrogacy exempted from child-selling statutes.

26. **WASHINGTON**: Criminalizes PAID surrogacy (gross misdemeanor); prohibits programs; contracts void; surrogate is mom and her husband, if she is married, is father.

27. **D.C.:** Prohibits contracts where surrogate is paid for termination of parental rights or consent to adoption; prohibits programs; $10,000 fine, 1 yr. jail.

28. **WISCONSIN**: Recognizes AI surrogacy; provides administrative mechanisms to get biological parents' names on birth certificate but refers to husband and wife as "adoptive parents."

Appendix 2
Information about SMI's program

SMI's Philosophy on Screening Surrogates:

If you have contacted surrogate programs other than Surrogate Mothers, Inc., you may have encountered different philosophies on screening surrogates before and during their pregnancies. Some programs, of course, do virtually no screening at all—*ever*. These are the programs that have had surrogates change their minds, or where couples or individuals ended up backing out of contracts or creating problems for the surrogates. In our program, all of our surrogates must be 18 - 35 and previously had children. Women fill out applications; they are interviewed over the phone; references are contacted; their medical records from their previous pregnancies are obtained; and then a profile sheet is prepared which summarizes their applications.

You then review those profile sheets and make a preliminary selection. It is at this point that our psychologist takes over and begins his formal screening of the surrogate. He contacts the surrogate over the phone, conducts a fairly detailed phone interview, interviews her references and sends me a letter with a recommendation as to whether the surrogate should come to Indianapolis for the full-blown testing. Assuming that she is acceptable up to this point, we arrange for the surrogate (and her husband if she is married) to come here. The psychological testing occurs over a weekend. I meet the surrogate at this time as well. You get a copy of the psychological report about two weeks after she is here. That report will give you a tremendous amount of information about the surrogate, her upbringing, her lifestyle, etc. You then make the final decision as to whether you would like to work with her, based on that report, all of the other information in her file which you are given and your meeting with her. After the decision is made to work with the surrogate and contracts are signed, we begin the medical procedures.

During the pregnancy SMI has a sort of "big sister" program set up where the women who have previously gone through the process are given the names of the surrogates who are going through it. Our surrogates very much enjoy talking to women who have previously delivered a child for another couple. While there is no formal psychological counseling that is required during the pregnancy, such counseling is available if the surrogates request it.

The reason we do not require formal counseling is quite simple. In the 26 years we have assisted couples with surrogacy, we have never had a woman change her mind. When we first began the program in 1984 and dealt only with local surrogates, we did have formal counseling during the pregnancy; and what we found was that our surrogates were offended by the idea that we did not think they were capable of handling the process without having a psychologist call them every month. It makes no sense to me, as the director of SMI, to say on the one hand that you will be trusting your surrogate with the most important thing in your life—the well being of your child—but on the other hand to say that you don't believe she is capable of performing that job without the assistance of a psychologist.

So, while SMI screens its surrogates as carefully as anyone in the country, we do not mandate that they attend counseling sessions during the pregnancy. It is not necessary; our surrogates don't like it; however, it is always available if the women think they could benefit from it. There are other programs that do have these mechanisms in place—one, for example, in California has only California surrogates who are *required* to attend monthly sessions; and we have actually heard from some of those women who said they wished they didn't have to do so.

Perhaps the best support our surrogates receive, other than from other surrogates, comes from our clients themselves. You will be meeting your surrogate and you'll have her phone number; and almost all of our surrogates like for you to be involved with them in the pregnancy. If SMI ever senses the need for your surrogate to speak to a psychologist, we will certainly let you know. Similarly, if you ever believe she could benefit from this, you should let us know.

We simply choose to treat our surrogates with the same degree of respect and dignity with which we treat our couples. No one forced you to undergo psychological counseling just because you chose to participate in surrogacy. We don't believe in *forcing* your surrogate to undergo counseling after she has already been determined to be emotionally, mentally and psychologically capable of carrying a child for you.

In order to assure ourselves and our clients that our surrogates are the most suitable women that can be found, we have a standard procedure we follow. A chart on the next page displays the steps of our program that, overall, eliminate 98% of the women who initially think they may be suitable surrogates—leaving only the best candidates for surrogacy that can be found anywhere in the industry to *carry your child.*

Surrogate Selection Process
Surrogate Mothers, Inc.

100 ■ Number of women, on average, who contact SMI every two weeks thinking they might want to be a surrogate.

20 ■ If the women contact us by phone, they must send a refundable $10 deposit to receive an application. If they contact us online, they must send a second, confirming email to receive an application. 80% of the women we hear from initially do not contact us again.

10 ■ The applications are long for two reasons. First, I want the surrogate (and her husband if she's married) to spend several hours reviewing the application to see how serious we are about what she's getting into; and second, the more information I can give my clients, the better informed they will be of their choices. 50% of the women who receive an application never return it.

5 ■ I review the application, contact the woman and interview her by phone. I try to be fairly liberal in my assessment of the surrogate because I want you to look at a number of profiles and have a sense of who is "good" and who isn't, I eliminate about half of the women I screen.

■ Once you choose a surrogate, we send her application to our psychologist. He contacts her, contacts her references and sends us a brief preliminary report as to whether she seems acceptable. He rejects 20% of the women he contacts.

■ If the woman is preliminarily acceptable, we then bring her to Indianapolis for the complete psychological screening. Whereas I try to be liberal in my initial assessment of the surrogate, we've instructed our psychologists to be conservative. I would always rather reject someone who is otherwise acceptable than the reverse. In the 25 years SMI has been doing this, our psychologists have rejected 50% of the women they've seen.

So, when all is said and done, only about 2% of the women who contact SMI actually end up in our program. This is the most rigorous screening in the industry, and it is the single most important reason why SMI has never had a case of failed surrogacy and is regarded as the most reputable surrogacy program in the world.

TIME TABLE

(For embryo transfer program)

The following time table will help you judge approximately how long it will take from the time that you select a surrogate until your child is born. These periods obviously are subject to change, but can be used as a general guideline.

1 - 4 weeks

Once the surrogate is selected, I will contact her to arrange for the psychological testing, which consists of several personality tests, marital relationship tests and an interview with the surrogate and her husband (if she is married).

3 - 8 weeks

Once the psychological screening is completed, the surrogate will be screened medically by the physicians responsible for the embryo transfer. We will have previously obtained and sent her medical history to them. After the medical screening, the doctors will determine if the surrogate is acceptable.

2-12 weeks

Assuming everything is okay with her physical, the surrogate will then sign the contracts. She is encouraged to obtain her own attorney, but this is not required.

Once the surrogate is selected, and possibly prior to selection, she will be taking her basal body temperature. The doctors doing the transfer like to have at least 2-3 temperature charts to assist them in predicting when the surrogate ovulates and, hence, when she is ready for the embryo transfer.

4 - 8 weeks

Once the surrogate has charted her temperature for a sufficient time, the doctors will request that she undergo blood tests called Estradials. These monitor the LH surge which occurs just before ovulation. She will have the tests performed for about 6 consecutive days starting on the 7th or 8th day of her cycle. At this point, the wife's cycle and the surrogate's cycle will be "matched" through the use of various drugs and/or birth control pills given to the wife.

3-5 days

After the surrogate's cycle and the wife's (or donor's) cycle are matched, the surrogate and the couple will go to the medical facility that has been chosen (in one of several different states depending on which program the couple is in) and the transfer will occur. This assumes that the wife responds adequately to the medication and that she has not ovulated too early. Occasionally, because of some type of problem, no transfer occurs.

Pregnancy tests are done about 2 weeks after the transfer. If the transfer is unsuccessful, the procedures will be repeated. If the transfer is successful, and a pregnancy occurs, the surrogate will be monitored by her own physician, and will deliver in about 8 months.

————

The total time, then, from initial surrogate selection until delivery will range from 15-18 months, assuming the surrogate conceives after the first transfer. The reason for such a wide range of time is that coordinating the cycles can be very difficult or relatively simple depending on a number of factors. Please consult the medical personnel at the facility you are using for answers to more specific medical questions.

CONFIDENTIAL
PARENTAL INTAKE FORM

Please fill out this form as accurately and truthfully as possible. Feel free to use extra space if necessary. Each applicant of a couple should fill out a separate form as all questions may not apply to each partner. *(Please copy blank form before beginning. You may enlarge if you wish.)*

I am:

_____ heterosexual and married;

_____ heterosexual and single;

_____ homosexual; involved with someone;

_____ homosexual and single

I am interested in selecting a surrogate for: *Check one.*

_____ the AI program only;

_____ the IVF/embryo transfer program only;

_____ the IVF/embryo transfer program primarily, but would consider the AI program as an option;

_____ the egg donor program

Name: _____

Maiden Name: _____

Address: _____

_____

_____

County of Residence: _____

Country of Residence: _____

Email address: _____

Home   Business

Phone: _____ Phone: _____

(Form continues on next page)

S.S.N.: _____-_____-_____ Date of Birth: _____/_____/_____

Place of Birth: _____

Height: ____ft. ____in.   Weight: _____lbs.

Race: _____   Religion: _____

Eyes: _____   Hair: _____   Blood Type: _____

Occupation: _____

Employer: _____

Years   Annual

Employed There: _____   Income: $_____

Medical and Family History

Date of Current Marriage: _____/____/_____

Where? _____

Dates of Previous Marriages/Divorces:

Married: ___/___/___ Divorced: ___/___/____

Married : ___/___/___ Divorced: ___/___/____

Number of children: ____

Names:	Ages:	(Natural (N)
		or Adopted (A)
_____	_____	_____
_____	_____	_____
_____	_____	_____

(Form continues on next page)

Please give a history of all pregnancies, regardless of whether or not they were full term. How did they end? (E.G., miscarriage, abortion, etc.)

_____

_____

_____

_____

What is the medical reason for your infertility?

_____

_____

_____

What doctors have you seen about infertility?

_____

_____

_____

_____

Do you or does anyone in your family have any known congenital diseases? If so, what are they?

_____

_____

_____

Have you ever been diagnosed as having AIDS or AIDS Related Complex?

YES _____   NO _____

(Form continues on next page)

Psycho-Social History

How do you feel about your (or your spouse's) infertility?

_____

_____

How has infertility affected your marriage?

_____

_____

Have you or you spouse ever seen a psychologist about your (or your spouse's) infertility? _____

Have you or your spouse ever seen a psychologist for any reason? _____

Have you ever been arrested or convicted of any crime (other than minor traffic offenses)? _____

If yes, explain briefly.

_____

_____

_____

Attitudes toward the Surrogate Procedure

Why have you chosen to have a child using the surrogate mother procedure?

_____

_____

_____

_____

(Form continues on next page)

What other alternative procedures have you tried (e.g. artificial insemination, in vitro, etc.)? What were the results?

_____

_____

Do you anticipate any emotional difficulties or reactions to the surrogate procedure? How do you think your spouse will answer this question?

My answer:

_____

_____

Spouse will say:

_____

_____

How will you feel having a child who is biologically related to one of you but not the other?

_____

_____

Do you plan to tell the child how it came into being? Why or why not?

_____

_____

Have you discussed the possibility that this child might be born with some sort of deformity? _____

What are the three most important characteristics to you that the surrogate possess (e.g. health, intelligence, religious/ethnic/race, athletic ability, physical characteristics, etc.)?

_____   _____

_____   _____

(Form continues on next page)

How do you think the surrogate will react to giving up the child?

_____

_____

If you had your choice, would you prefer the child to be male or female?   _____

Attitudes toward the Surrogate

Do you want to meet the surrogate?   _____

Do you want to know her by name?   _____

What kind of relationship would you like to have with your surrogate, both during and after the pregnancy?

_____

_____

Do you have any objections to publicity about your involvement in the program?   If so, do you have any objections to publicity if no identifying information about you is revealed?

_____

_____

If the fetus were determined to be in some respect abnormal, would you want the surrogate to abort the child?

_____

On a separate page, please list or explain anything that I have not covered, or that you think is especially important. Also, please briefly describe your background, where and how you were raised, how you met your spouse, your education, etc. Plus, we will need a list of three references other than family members who we can contact.

(Form continues on next page)

With this application, please include a picture of you (and your spouse if applicable) and a non-refundable application fee of $500.00.

Signature: _____

Date: _____/_____/_____

AFFIDAVIT

I/We,

_____,

(hereinafter referred to as "Applicant" whether jointly or singly), after being first duly sworn, do state as follows:

1. Applicant certifies that applicant is seeking information about the surrogate mother program to which an application ahs been made and that the purpose for such application is to be considered as a surrogate or to work with a surrogate. Applicant certifies that truthful information has been submitted to Surrogate Mothers, Inc. (SMI) with the good faith intention of participating in the surrogate program and not as a member of any media or on behalf of any third party.

2. Applicant further certifies that he/she/they have never been charged with or convicted of a: 1) any crime of violence or any felony; 2) any crime of a sexual nature; 3) any allegation, charge or conviction, either of a criminal or civil nature, involving abuse or neglect of any person.

FURTHER AFFIANT SAYETH NOT

Potential Surrogate: _____

Potential Surrogate's Husband: _____

Wife of Couple: _____

Husband of Couple: _____

State of _____

County of _____

Before me a notary public in and for said County and State, personally appeared

_____,
who after being first duly sworn acknowledged the previous affidavit and stated that the representations therein were true and accurate.

My Commission expires: ____/____/____

_____
Notary Public

I am often contacted by couples who have their own surrogate. If you need legal assistance with your own surrogacy arrangement, we are happy to provide it. Below is the application to complete if you already have your own surrogate and simply need us to complete your contracts and other legal work.

FOR CLIENTS WHO HAVE THEIR OWN SURROGATE

CONFIDENTIAL PARENTAL INTAKE FORM

Please fill out this form as accurately and truthfully as possible. Each applicant of a married couple **and your surrogate and her husband** should fill out a separate form (***Please copy blank form before beginning. May enlarge if you wish.***) as all questions may not apply to each spouse. (Your surrogate does not have to complete the financial information questions.) For couples, please provide your name exactly as you wish it to appear on the birth certificate.

Name: _____

Maiden Name: _____

Address: _____

_____

County of Residence: _____

Country of Residence: _____

(Form continues on next page)

Email: _____

Home Phone: _____

Business Phone: _____

SSN: _____-____-____ Date of Birth: ____/____/_____

Place of birth: _____

Occupation: _____

Employer: _____

Years Employed There: _____ Annual Income: $_____

Date of Current Marriage: _____

Where Married: _____

Dates of Previous Marriages/Divorces:

_____

_____

Number of Children: _____

Names   Ages: Natural (N)—Adopted (A)

_____

_____

_____

Type of Surrogacy:

_____ Artificial Insemination _____Embryo   Transfer

(Form continues on next page)

If you are in the AI program, what is the full name you wish the child to have after the adoption is finalized?

_____

Date of Surrogate's Pregnancy: _____

Date of delivery: _____

Has Surrogate's husband had a vasectomy? _____

If so, when? _____

Has paternity been established? _____

(If so, please include a copy of the court order.)

Who is/are the biological parents of the child the surrogate is carrying?

_____

_____

SMI IS PROUD TO INTRODUCE THE

PLATINUM SERVICE LEVEL—

AN UNPARALLELED COMMITMENT TO ENSURING THAT YOUR NEEDS ARE MET IMMEDIATELY AND WITHOUT EXCEPTION

SMI is proud to announce the availability of an exclusive, never-before-offered opportunity for a select few clients who demand the highest levels of service and satisfaction—

the PLATINUM SERVICE LEVEL

We at SMI have always believed that our clients—YOU—are entitled to the most professional service available anywhere in the world. After all, you are entrusting us with the future well being of your child; indeed, the very existence of a new baby brought into your lives!

Since we began in 1984, we have strived to distinguish our surrogacy program from any other in the world by delivering a personal, caring touch to the services we offer you. As the world's most reputable surrogacy program, we believe that we have accomplished that goal; and we continue to provide every one of our clients with the most attention, the most communication—both prior to and throughout your surrogate's pregnancy—and the most compassion for you and your surrogate available anywhere.

At the heart of SMI's philosophy is the idea that our clients demand and are unquestionably entitled to the utmost respect. For a select few of you, we are committed to raising that bar even higher, and offering the most personalized, all-inclusive surrogacy package available on the planet. Make no mistake—for **every one of you** the legal work we do will ensure that your rights are solidly protected and that you will never have to be concerned about the "what ifs" so many people wonder about. For some of you, however, we are prepared to offer the following incentives, above and beyond everything else we do:

➢ Your own dedicated toll free phone number, *available to you and you alone*, with our GUARANTEE that if we cannot answer your question immediately, Steven Litz, SMI's founder and president, will personally return your phone call by the next business day.

➢ Your personal concierge who will handle every one of your travel needs: booking flights and hotels, arranging all transportation and transfers for you, even ensuring that you are met at the airport by someone knowledgeable about the city you're travelling to.

➤ FREE limousine travel to/from the clinic or hotel at your request.

➤ A FREE in-person U.S. consultation with Mr. Litz so that you never have to worry about what to expect next and so that your busy schedule is not interrupted by having to travel to Indianapolis. *He'll come to you!*

➤ FREE local counsel fees for any legal work that needs to be done on your behalf.

➤ A FREE car seat waiting for you at the hospital when you pick up your baby.

If this sounds interesting to you, when you sign your contract with SMI, simply check *the box that says you wish to receive the $10,000 platinum upgrade.* This will change your initial investment from $20,000 to $30,000, and SMI's advertising fee from $5000 to $15,000. All other fees remain the same—and you'll be pampered along your journey with the most luxurious services available!

INQUIRY FORM

For further information, including a complete packet which contains contracts, pamphlets, magazine articles and a full application to the program, please complete the following form. You may mail it, fax it, or Email it to:

Surrogate Mothers, Inc.
Steven C. Litz, Director
PO Box 216
Monrovia, IN 46157
(317) 996-2000
(317) 996-2033 (fax)
scl@surrogatemothers.com (Email)

☐ YES—please send me more information about your program. There is no cost or obligation.

Name: _____

Address:

_____

_____

_____

Email: _____

or

☐ YES—please call me.

Phone: _____

You may also access all of this information by visiting our website at:

www.surrogatemothers.com

or

You can complete an application online through our website at:

http://www.surrogatemothers.com/parental_application.html

"3 free resources from Surrogate Mothers Inc"

Access Online at www.FindASurrogate.com

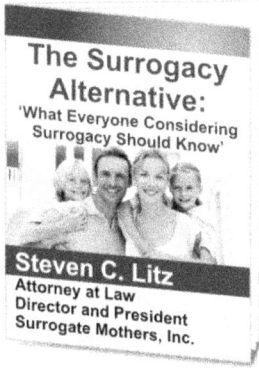

The Surrogacy Alternative:

"What Everyone Considering Surrogacy Should Know."

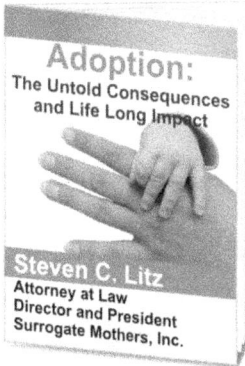

Adoption:

The Untold Consequences
and
Life Long Impact

The Surrogate Mothers, Inc.

Information and
How-To Guide

www.ingramcontent.com/pod-product-compliance
Lightning Source LLC
Chambersburg PA
CBHW021342090426
42742CB00008B/698